WRIGLEY'S WAN
A Tail of Adventure in Atlanta

Written by Meghan Roessler

Illustrated by QBN Studios

MW01153145

Copyright © 2024 by Meghan Roessler
Illustrated by QBN Studios

All rights reserved. No part of this book may be reproduced in any form or by any electronic or mechanical means, including information storage and retrieval systems, without permission in writing from the publisher, except by reviewers, who may quote brief passages in a review.

To the shelter dogs who have tails full of stories and hearts full of dreams - this book is for you and the magical moments yet to come!

A portion of the proceeds from all books sold will benefit a Georgia-based rescue or shelter.

A native of Georgia, a state in the South,
Wrigley the dog is famous, no doubt!

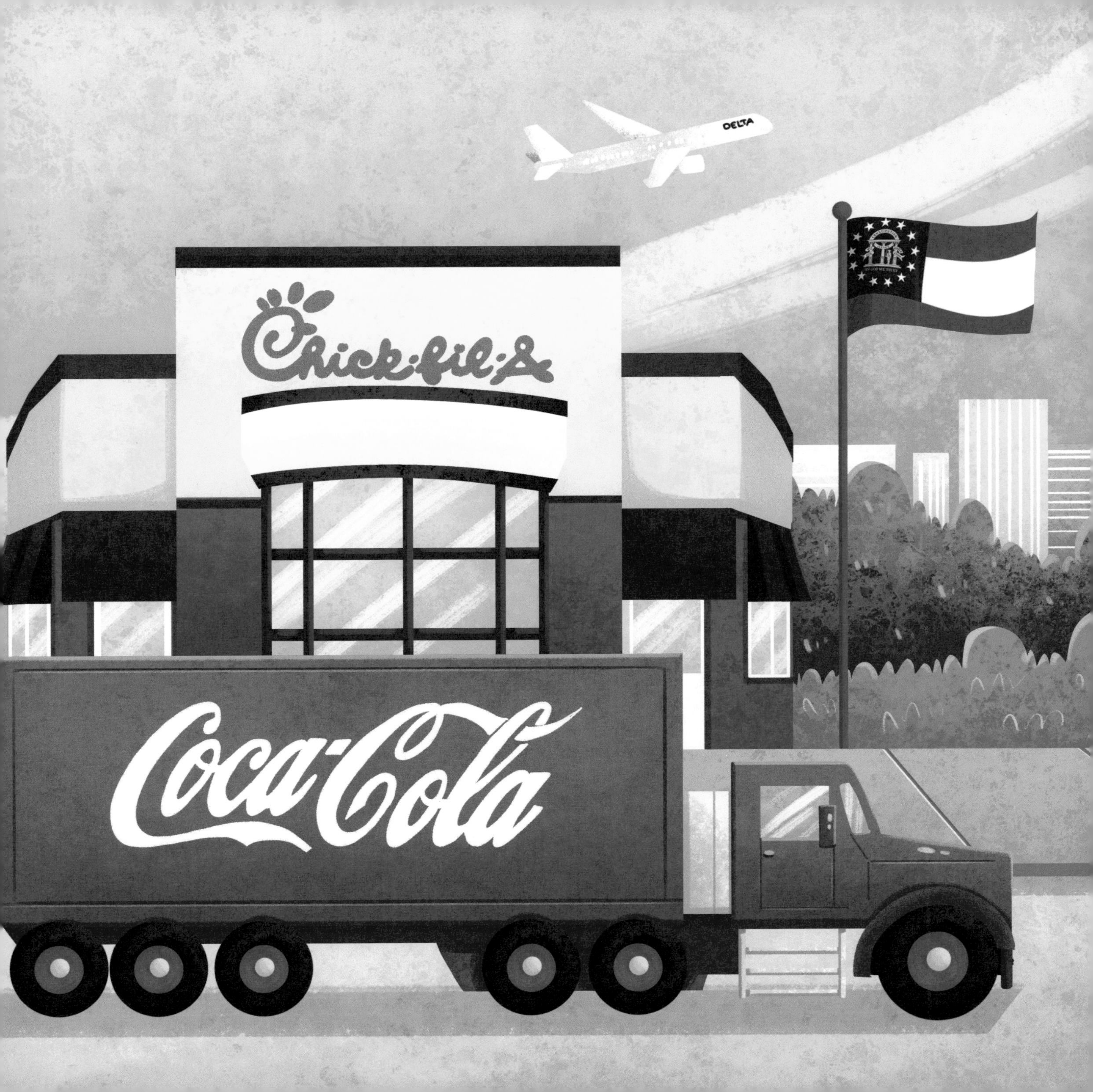
DELTA
Chick-fil-A
Coca-Cola

He's smart and he's kind, he's dapper and sweet,
He's everyone's best friend who will give him a treat!

He's a handsome young boy whose coat is brown and black,
His breed was found to be super-mutt when he got his DNA test back!

He lives outside Atlanta, not far from downtown,
He's always exploring from sun up to sun down.

So many spots to see, so many sniffs to be had,
He's toured lots of places as a young lad!

He loves summer days down on the Hooch,
He swims and catches a tan – he's one stylish pooch!

Lunch at Mellow Mushroom or McCray's is the move,
A place that's dog friendly he will always approve!

Barking Dog
Bakery & Feed

No day out is complete without a stop to The Barking Dog Bakery and Feed,
It's the best place in town for chews and sweet treats indeed!

Miss Betsy is his favorite, she makes all the cakes,
She's not afraid to toss a sample his way when she bakes!

He loves to play fetch and run all around,
One of his favorite spots to play is Piedmont
Park downtown.

He rides down in the car with his parents to play,
He knows at this point he will be out and about all day!

Different dogs to be seen – both big and small,
All just as ready as he is to chase after the tennis ball!

He chases and plays with each dog he can find,
Once he's there for a few hours, it's time to unwind.

He goes to the Battery to walk all around,
During baseball season, this is the hot spot
to watch the Braves throw down!

Appetizers and dinner at Antico or Live,
children old and young come by to high five!

His eyes get tired, he's had a long day,
He rests on the way home to go sleep the night away!

He takes off his collar and lies on the bed,
Dreams of fun in Atlanta run around in his head!

Wrigley Roessler
338 Fly the W Dr.
Atlanta, GA 30339

He'll wake up in the morning
and be ready to roll,
To tackle a new tourist spot –
his heart will be full!
Atlanta is awesome, there's
much to see and do,
If you come and visit, Wrigley
can be your tour guide too!

Goodbye from Georgia

Love, WRIGLEY

MEET THE AUTHOR

Meghan Roessler is a wife and dog mom that lives in Canton, GA with her husband, Brad, and handsome rescue-mutt and inspiration for this book, Wrigley! Meghan and Brad met in Chicago when she was in graduate school and the two not only fell in love; but also, fell in love with cheering on the Chicago Cubs. When they adopted Wrigley in June 2020 from a rescue in Newnan, GA, the name instantly fit his personality. Wrigley has truly changed their lives and has inspired friends and family across the country to follow his travels and celebration of daily national holidays. Meghan hopes that this book will continue to raise awareness of the millions of dogs that wait in shelters and rescues across the country to find their fur-ever homes.

The Roesslers love to cheer on the Cleveland Browns, Philadelphia Eagles, The Ohio State University Buckeyes, the Georgia Bulldogs, the Atlanta Braves and of course, the Chicago Cubs!

Meghan is a native of Northeast Ohio and attended Akron St. Vincent - St. Mary High School, earned a BS Biology and was a four-year basketball player for the Blue Streaks at John Carroll University (University Heights, OH) and earned her Master of Higher Education Administration from North Park University (Chicago, IL).

To stay up to date with Wrigley and his latest adventures, follow him on Instagram @wrigleytheatldog

Made in the USA
Columbia, SC
24 October 2024

45007359R00018